Bush Walkabout

Bush Walkabout

AXEL POIGNANT

⯅ ADDISON-WESLEY

 **An Addisonian Press Book**

HA/HO   6/74   05854

Library of Congress Cataloguing in Publication
Data

Poignant, Axel.
   Bush walkabout.

   SUMMARY: Photographs accompany the
account of the adventures of two Aborigine
children who wander into the bush and become
lost.
   "An Addisonian Press book."
   First published in 1957 under title: Piccaninny
walkabout.
   A translation of an Aborigine tale by Raiwalla
as told to B. Lowe.
   1. Australian aborigines—Juvenile literature
[1. Australian aborigines] I. Raiwalla.
II. Lowe, Beulah. III. Title.
GN665.P64   1974   398.2'0994
73-20026
ISBN 0 201 05854 5

First published in this edition 1974
by Addison-Wesley, Reading, Mass., U.S.A.

Introduction

IN 1952 after a stay of some months on the coast of Arnhem Land I visited the mission station on Milingimbi Island. I watched the Aborigine children at the mission school and was fascinated by them.

A few days after my arrival, school holidays started. Some of the children went walkabout with their parents to the mainland, but others stayed at Milingimbi and played all day in the bush and on the beach. They were so alive, so intelligent and eager in their response to Miss Beulah Lowe, their teacher, that I wanted to convey something of their life with my camera.

I began making up a story about them and the adventures that might befall two children during the course of a day. Finally I read my neatly typed story to Raiwalla, an Aborigine who acted as interpreter and had agreed to help me with my photographic project. I had not read more than half a dozen lines when Raiwalla politely interrupted me, saying, "I will tell you the story". He promptly began to tell a story which I am bound to admit was far superior to my own.

But Raiwalla had difficulty in telling the story in understandable English, so Miss Lowe who is an expert at Gubabuingu, Raiwalla's language, came and helped. She wrote down the story in his own words and later translated it into English for me.

In all honesty, therefore, I cannot claim to be the author of the tale told in this book. The adventures of Nullagundi and Rikili, two very real children, might well be called an Aboriginal bedtime story, and it is actually told to children around the camp-fire at night.

Nullagundi, the boy, is about ten years old. Rikili, the girl, is about nine. They are typical of the laughing, happy children found in Arnhem Land.

For Nullagundi this was his last year as a "child". The time was at hand when he would enter manhood. Indeed it was only a short time after the pictures in this book were taken that he went through the first and most important of the initiations that would make him a man. In Arnhem Land this first initiation occurs at any time between the age of seven and ten. As soon as these ceremonies begin, life becomes very different for the boy concerned. He may no longer speak to his sister or many of the other women who are closely related to him. Taboos are imposed on him. There are foods that he may not eat, and his behaviour is strictly controlled.

The girl, on the other hand, just goes on growing up. The course of her life is pretty much pre-ordained for her. Sometimes girls are promised in marriage even before they are born. Rikili, the girl of our story, has already been promised and will be claimed by her husband as soon as she is old enough. This is in accordance with ancient custom, which, incidentally, is changing nowadays.

Australian Aborigines are indulgent towards their children, pet them and spoil them, but the hard facts of life are implicit in their games. And when the mission children go walkabout with their parents they continue their education in Aboriginal lore. They learn how to keep alive in country where an inexperienced white man would perish in a few days.

On these walkabouts the children are constantly taught the skills necessary for a life in the bush: how to find food and water, how to hunt and fish, how to construct a bark canoe, how to weave a basket and to make a spear.

Very important, too, are the songs and stories they hear around the camp-fire at night. These tell of their ancestors, of how the world was made, and of all the legends and mysteries associated with their culture. Also round the camp-fire, often in song and dance, are retold the adventures of the day just ended.

On special occasions the Aborigines paint wonderful and meaningful patterns on their bodies. The ritual ceremonies, commonly called corroborees, which they then perform may last for several days and even for weeks. Many ceremonies are secret, and women and children are not permitted to watch them. Women, too, have a ritual life of their own, and the males of the tribe are not permitted to see their corroborees.

The younger children go food-gathering with the womenfolk. They learn all the skills of finding food and are taught how to track animals and read the signs of the bush. When the tide is out the women and children spend much of their time looking for oysters and other shellfish. Worms are found in the roots of the salt-water mangroves, and one of my photographs shows a girl holding a piece of mangrove root from which she has just pulled out a worm. These worms are beautifully coloured, shading from pink to reddish purple. Rikili, in the same photograph, holds a number of worms in a paperbark container.

The paperbark-tree has a very soft, pliable bark that can be pulled off the tree in large sheets. The Aborigines cover their spearheads with this bark and use it to wrap up special objects. It is also used to wrap up the dead. Various articles, such as dilly-bags, are made from the fibres of the pandanus palm leaf. Sometimes these dillybags are so well made that they would hold water. They are used for food-gathering and to carry things on walkabout.

Another kind of bark is used for canoe-making.

In Arnhem Land the Aborigines make two kinds of canoe. One is the hollowed-out log of a tree, made in accordance with the method that was introduced into the country by the Macassar traders long ago. And the ancient aboriginal canoe is made as it has been made for thousands of years, from the bark of a eucalypt called the stringybark. A piece of bark, which may be from twelve to fourteen feet long, is cut off in one piece. It is flattened and softened until it can be bent inside out, and is then held with sticks in the general shape of a canoe. After that the ends are sewn together with vines. Two poles are lashed along the edges to make the canoe more rigid.

Most fishing is done with a fish-spear that has four or five prongs on the end of a shaft. For bigger game like turtle or dugong a harpoon is used. Small fish like the ones Nullagundi brings to his grandmother are put straight on the hot ashes without gutting, but fish as big as the ones which the three men are carrying must be gutted first. The manner of cooking these larger fish is also different. A shallow pit is scooped out and a good fire is built in it with sticks. On top of the sticks a number of stones are placed. The fire is lit and allowed to burn down. A bed is then made of heated stones. The fish is placed on them and covered with more hot stones. A piece of paperbark is placed over the stones, and this in turn is covered with earth. And as the Aborigines say, "You leave it a little bit long time" —say about half an hour—after which it is ready for eating. And very good, too!

As soon as they can walk the boys start throwing toy spears at small animals and fish, all the time practising and improving their skill. When a little older they play a game with spears, as the children in the story do. This game is a preparation for later life, when they will probably have to take part in what is called a "peace-making ceremony". When a big corroboree is about to take place, steps are taken to ensure that there shall be peace and harmony throughout. All animosities must be settled. For example, if a man has killed someone and the dead man's brothers and other relatives arrive at the same place as the killer, the corroboree may not take place until "peace" has been made. So the relatives of the dead man meet the "killer" and throw spears at him in accordance with strict rules. The accused may not throw his own spear, but may use it to deflect the avenging party's spears. If he manages to escape being hit, he will at the end of the ordeal approach the other party with prescribed dancing steps, and one of them will jab at his thigh with a spear. Blood has now been spilt and the need for vengeance is satisfied. On the other hand the accused may have been hit and injured during the spear-throwing, in which case the grudge is considered settled, and the important work of the corroboree can go on in peace.

Naturally Nullagundi takes his spear and woomera (or spear-thrower) with him on the adventure described in this story. He uses them when he hunts the wallaby. The spear-thrower is a long flat piece of shaped wood with a small hook on the end; this hook fits into a hollow in the end of the spear and gives greater extension and leverage in the act of throwing. Throwing and aiming in this fashion take a great deal of skill, but the woomera enormously increases the force of the throw.

No man can travel very far without water, and the Australian Aborigine is extremely skilful in finding it. Very often he finds water in a "soak" in a creek-bed. A hole is dug and the water lying beneath the surface of the earth seeps into it. When this story was photographed there had been no rain for two years and water was very hard to find. When it was suggested that the children get some water out of a tree, I could hardly believe they were serious, but a paperbark-tree was selected and a spot on the trunk chosen where Nullagundi bruised it with a stone. The water came out in a steady series of big drops, till some two cupfuls were collected. It was slightly brackish in taste, but welcome indeed to the thirsty!

The shelter which Nullagundi builds is very simple; it consists of a few stakes and some sheets of paperbark. Its purpose is to keep out the cold wind and the dew. The family shelter shown at the beginning of the story is made of a few thick pieces of stringybark. Two shallow trenches are dug several feet apart and the bark is bent over so that its ends rest in the trenches. One end of the shelter is closed with a sheet of paperbark to keep out the wind. This type of shelter is used only at the end of the dry season, when there are only occasional showers. As a rule nearly everybody sleeps on the ground outside, moving into the shelter only when it rains. When the rainy season starts, the Aborigines build larger huts to shelter the entire family.

You would think Nullagundi too big to be carried back to the camp on his father's shoulders, but to children who normally sleep in the protection of the family circle a night alone in the bush would be a most fearsome experience. To them the darkened bush is a place filled with supernatural and menacing forces.

Their safe return, therefore, is celebrated with a camp corroboree.

AXEL POIGNANT

Sydney,
September 1956

IN Arnhem Land on the northern coast of
Australia, there live two Aborigine children.
They are brother and sister and their names are . . .

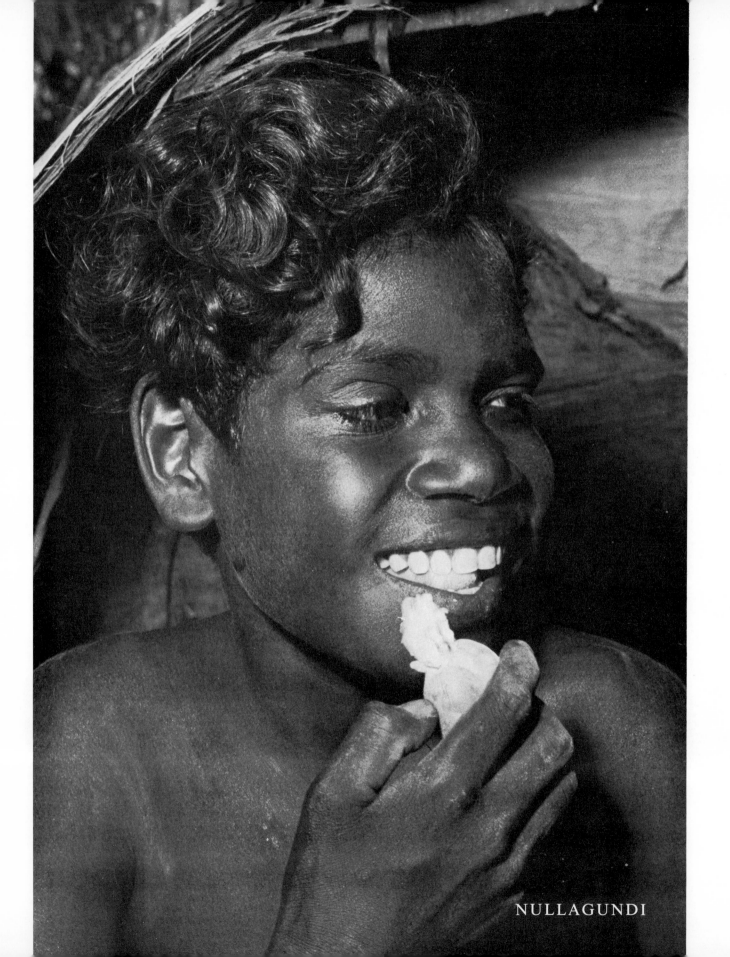

NULLAGUNDI

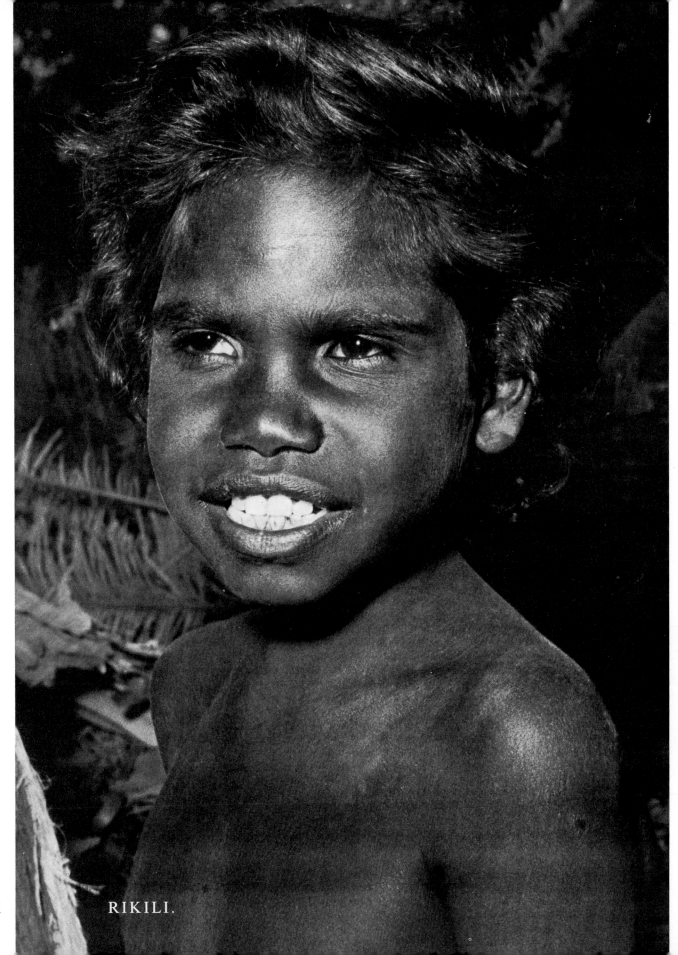

and   RIKILI.

Early one morning while the children were still asleep Father and Mother prepared to go hunting.

Father said to the grandmother, "Here's some food for the children. We are going hunting for honey, yams, roots and berries, kangaroo, emu and goose. I will get the meat, and Mother will find the bush foods. Will you look after the children, please?"

"All right," she said. "You go hunting and bring back something good."

Father and Mother set off, leaving Grandmother with the children. Soon the children woke up and looked around for their parents.

"Where's Mother?" they asked.

"She has gone to get us some food," said Grandmother.

"And Father?" said Nullagundi.

"He's gone hunting, too."

"What is there to eat now?"

"Here you are," said Grandmother. "Cycad nuts, honey and some meat. Hurry up and eat them. Then you may go and play."

Rikili and another little girl wandered along the beach together.

But Rikili was still hungry so they took their digging sticks and dilly bags and joined some other people who were gathering shellfish on the beach.

Afterwards they went in search of the tasty worms that live in the roots of mangrove-trees.

They found plenty and had a fine feast.

Nullagundi and his friends wandered around the camp, making sure they missed nothing that was going on. They watched the basket being woven and the spear being sharpened. One of the men had gathered his spears ready for hunting. And some of the others were very busy making a bark canoe that they would use when they went out fishing with their spears.

Then Nullagundi and a playmate went walking
along the shore.

They saw some fish in the water and wondered
what kind of fish they were. Nullagundi's
playmate looked carefully.

"They should be good to eat," he said.

"I'll go and get Father's fish-spear," said
Nullagundi.

They speared some of the fish and Nullagundi
took his share to his grandmother.

"Will you cook these for me? I'm going back to
play."

As Grandmother took them, she thought to
herself, "He's so small, yet he is trying to be a
great hunter!"

Soon Nullagundi returned.

"Where are my fish, Grandmother?"

"Here they are, my boy."

"Will you have some?" he said.

"No, thank you, my boy. You're still a child.
You need plenty of food to make you big and
strong. When you grow up into a man, then
certainly I'll eat what you catch."

Rikili and her friend had found a nest of wild bees at the top of a tree. They were not afraid to rob the nest of its honey, for the wild bee has no sting and cannot harm anyone.

Rikili went in search of Nullagundi and, when she found him, showed him the nuts and shellfish that she had gathered.

Then she said, "What game shall we play now?"

"Let's have a spear-fight," said Nullagundi.

They called their friends and asked them to join
in the game.

"All right," said one boy. "But we'll have to tie
soft bark round the points of our spears, so that
no one will get hurt."

"Good," said Nullagundi. "You and I will be the
two fighters, and the other two can hold us back,
just like grown-ups in a real fight."

"Yes, the girls can stand between us and try to
hit our spears to stop us from killing each other.
If anyone gets hurt they can sit around and cry."

So the boys made some toy spears, carefully
wrapping paperbark round the pointed ends.
Then they threw the spears at each other, and the
two girls stood between them and tried to hit
the flying spears.

At last one of the boys pretended to be killed.
The killer ran away, and the girls wept over the
victim, throwing themselves on the ground,
hitting their heads with stones, and crying loudly.

Afterwards they said, "Let's go for a swim." They all ran into the sea.

And Rikili and her friend caught a big mangrove crab.

Rikili's little friend put on a garland of flowers.
But Rikili grew tired of all these games and went
off to find her brother.

"What do you want now?" he said.

"We could go and look for Mother and Father," said Rikili.
"I think they went to the lagoon."
"But Grandmother will see us," said Nullagundi.
"We could go the other way round."
"That's a good idea!"

So the children went off into the bush.

They had not gone far when Rikili said, "I'm hungry again. What about catching a bird or a goanna, Nullagundi? A bandicoot would do. Just something to eat before we go any farther. Look! There's a wallaby! See if you can spear it."

But the wallaby was too clever for them. He jumped away before Nullagundi had time to throw his spear. The children went on through the bush, all the time looking for something that they could catch and eat.

"There. Nullagundi! A goanna! In the log! I can see his tail."

"You're right," said Nullagundi, getting ready to grab it. "Move out of my way, and find a stick and poke him from the other end. I'll pull him by the tail."

"All right, but hold him properly," said Rikili. "Be careful he doesn't bite you."

"Yes, yes, I know."

Rikili prodded, and the boy pulled with all his might until the goanna came out of the log. He killed it at once.

"How are we going to light a fire to cook it, Nullagundi?"

"I'll make some firesticks and try rubbing them together as Father does."

"You *are* brave and strong," said Rikili.

"Come on, little sister, you help me and it won't take long."

"No, brother, you do it. My hands are too tender. Anyway, I'm so hungry, I think I'll eat it raw."

"Don't be silly. You go and collect some firewood. I'll try to make the fire, and we'll soon have it cooked."

After several attempts the sticks started to smoke, and Nullagundi tipped the smouldering powder on to some dry grass and blew gently. Soon the grass was alight and he set fire to the wood that Rikili had gathered. He then put the goanna in the fire to cook it.

"Is it cooked yet, Nullagundi?"

"Nearly, little sister."

"Hurry up and turn it over."

"In a minute, when this side is done."

When the goanna was cooked, Nullagundi pulled it off the fire and threw it on the ground to cool. Then, in no time, the children ate it up.

"Come on, Rikili, we *must* find Mother and Father. It is getting late. Maybe they have caught some fish. Shall we go this way?"

"This is the place," said Nullagundi. "But where is their fire?"

"There isn't one," she said.

"Well, Grandmother said they were coming here," said Nullagundi. "I wonder where they have gone? We must try somewhere else. Maybe over there? Come on, let's go and see."

But not a soul was to be seen.

"There is nobody here either," said Rikili, "and the sun is nearly set. Do you know where we are, Nullagundi?"

"No, little sister. I am afraid we have come the wrong way."

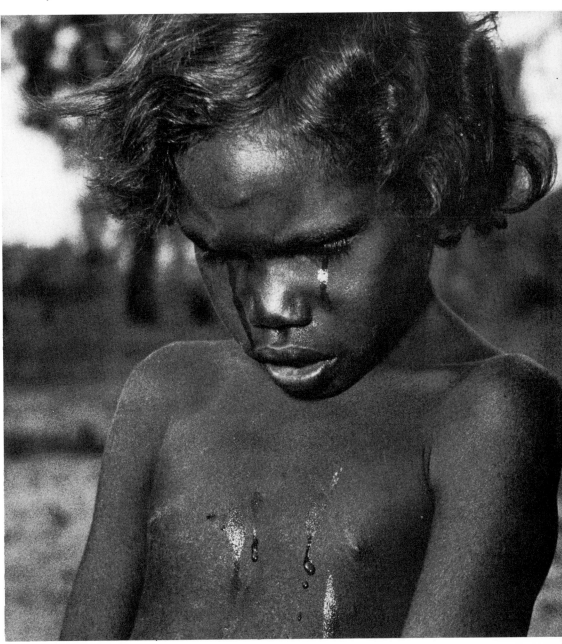

Rikili began to cry. "What are we going to do? It is almost night time and the camp is a long way off. How are we going to get home?"

"I'm not sure," said Nullagundi.

"Then why did you bring me so far? I'm very thirsty," she said. "I thought you knew where we were going."

"So I did. But I don't know where we are now.
We should have followed the proper track.
You were the one who made me come away from
Grandmother. Well, I'll find some water for you,
and then we had better find a place to camp.

"Come on, Rikili, don't cry. We may find some
water if we dig in this creek-bed. This looks a likely place."

"Hurry up and dig, and we'll see," said Rikili.

Nullagundi dug, but because there had been no
rain for a long time he found no water.

They walked a little farther.

"Look! There is a water-tree," cried Nullagundi.
"Perhaps we will find some water there. Let's
find a sharp stone to hit the tree with; you make a
paperbark cup to catch the water, Rikili."

"No, you do it, brother. I'm only a little girl."

So Nullagundi made the cup.

"There you are, sister. Now I'll hit the tree.
When it cracks, the water will trickle out. You be
ready to catch it."

Nullagundi hit the tree, and water soon dripped
out and filled the cup.

"Shall I drink it?" asked Rikili.

"Yes, go on. But let me have some too."

"Here you are, brother."

"Just a minute," he said. "Get out of the way. I'll
hit the tree again and get some more water. There
you are. Now you can cool your skin with it."

And the children used up all the water. . . .

Nullagundi prepared a camp for the night. He stuck some sticks into the ground in a semi-circle and tied the tops together to form the framework for a shelter. He then peeled enough bark from the paperbark-trees to cover the framework, and with his firesticks he made a small fire to keep them warm through the night.

"Sleep well, little sister. I'll look after you," said Nullagundi.

When Mother and Father returned to the camp it was dark and they were surprised that the children did not run to meet them. They put down their spears and the food they had gathered and said, "Where are the children, Grandmother?"

"They disappeared," she said, "and I thought they must have gone after you. I hope nothing terrible has happened."

She and everyone else were very worried, for it was now too dark to see the children's tracks. Then somebody said, "I saw them this morning. I think they went that way."

"We shall start looking for them as soon as it gets light," said Father.

Early next morning Rikili and Nullagundi got up feeling very glad it was daylight once again. Nullagundi straightened his spear so that his aim would be good when hunting. He told Rikili to pick up a piece of burning wood from the fire.

"We shall light a big fire so that Mother and Father will be able to see the smoke and know where to find us," said Nullagundi.

Mother and Father had set out early to find the children. It was not long before Mother called out, "Here are their footprints, and the grass is bent back here. This is the way they went."

"Let's call out. Perhaps they are not far away." They called, but nobody answered.

"Look!" cried Father. "Over there! It's smoke, a long way off."
"They must have lit a fire. Let's hurry!"

As they hurried towards the fire, Father found the place where the children had dug in the creek-bed. "They must have been looking for water!" he exclaimed.

"No, it must have been some grown-ups."

"No, here are their footprints. These are Nullagundi's and those are Rikili's."

"Well, they didn't find any water here," said Mother. "I do hope they're both all right."

"Ah, there's a water-tree. It looks as though they got some water from it. They must have been hot and thirsty."

"Here are some more footprints."

"Where are they going to?"

"They are pointing back towards the sea."

"But here are some more going the other way. I'll hurry on ahead," said Father. And he ran through the bush, calling out all the time.

Far away, the two children heard a faint sound.

"Listen, brother," said Rikili.

"That's only a bird," said Nullagundi.

"No, it's not. I can hear some people."

Nullagundi called again as loudly as he could. "A-a-a-a-a-ah. . . ."

"Call again, Nullagundi," said Rikili. And he gave an extra loud cry.

"You call too, little sister."

"No, I'm not big enough."

So Nullagundi cried out again.

This time Father heard him clearly, and he came running forward, shouting, "Is that you, Nullagundi? Where is your sister? Are you all right?"

"Here she is. She is sitting in the shade of a tree."

Picking up the two children, Father carried them back to Mother. "Let's get back to camp, and give them some food and water."

As they approached the camp they called out, "We've found them!"

Everybody embraced the children and cried for joy. Grandmother took the little girl from her mother's arms and hugged her.

The children were given yams, honey, fish, nuts and kangaroo meat. They ate until they could eat no more.

That day Grandmother made up her mind that she would always watch them very closely, while they were in her care.

Their friends and relations were so happy to see Nullagundi and Rikili home safe and sound that they decided to have a big corroboree to celebrate their return. Everyone danced and sang, and as the children danced with them the smiles on their painted faces showed how glad they were to be home from their walkabout.

Acknowledgments

It would have been impossible to photograph this little
story if it had not been for the invaluable help given not
only by Miss Beulah Lowe but also by the Reverend
A. F. Ellemor, who at the time of my stay on Milingimbi
Island was Chairman of the North Australia District of
the Methodist Overseas Mission, and his devoted staff
and helpers on their mission stations. They put up with
the inconvenience of having me around while coping
with their own problems: problems of helping Aborigines
and white people to understand each other and so smooth
a vital transition period. Australians can be proud of their
fine effort. I would also like to thank the Rt. Hon. Sir
Paul Hasluck, Governor-General of Australia, who was
then Minister for Territories, for his help in making this
venture possible.

A.P.

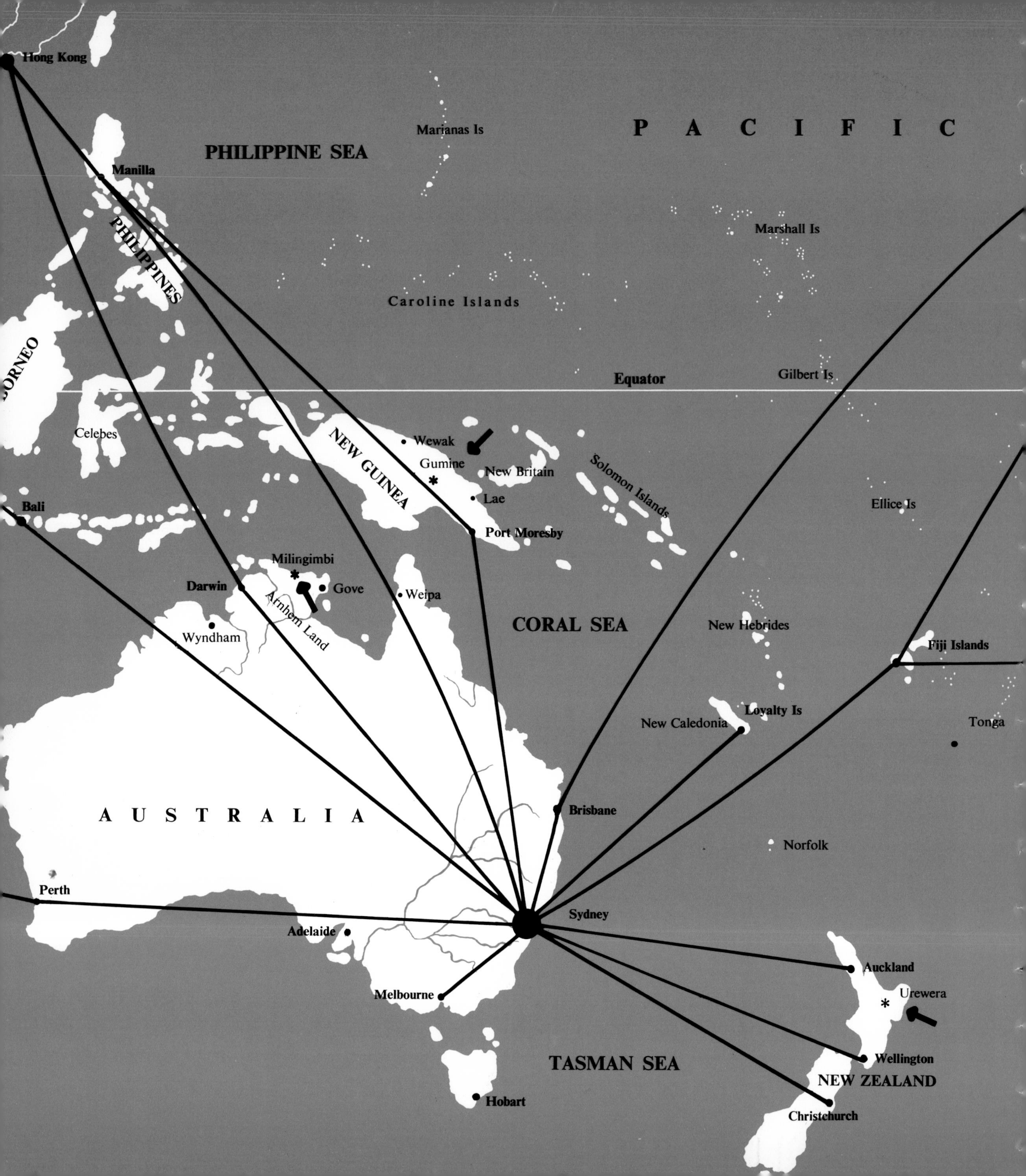

Hong Kong
Marianas Is
P A C I F I C
PHILIPPINE SEA
Manilla
PHILIPPINES
Marshall Is
Caroline Islands
BORNEO
Equator
Gilbert Is
Celebes
NEW GUINEA
Wewak
Gumine
New Britain
Solomon Islands
Lae
Ellice Is
Bali
Port Moresby
Milingimbi
Darwin
Gove
Weipa
Arnhem Land
Wyndham
CORAL SEA
New Hebrides
Fiji Islands
Loyalty Is
New Caledonia
Tonga
Brisbane
A U S T R A L I A
Norfolk
Perth
Sydney
Adelaide
Auckland
Urewera
Melbourne
TASMAN SEA
Wellington
NEW ZEALAND
Hobart
Christchurch